Key to the Philosophy of Immaterialism

George Lowell Tollefson

PALO FLECHADO PRESS

Copyright © 2024 George Lowell Tollefson in *Thoughts on Creativity, Spirit, and the Ethical Life*

All rights reserved.

ISBN: 978-1-952026-10-2

Palo Flechado Press, Santa Fe, New Mexico

OTHER PHILOSOPHICAL WORKS BY GEORGE LOWELL TOLLEFSON

Thoughts on Creativity, Spirit, and the Ethical Life

The Immaterial Structure of Human Experience
The Limits of Reason
The Thinking Process

Unbridled Democracy

A Healer of Nations

Extracts from *Unbridled Democracy*
Spirit as Universal Consciousness
The Thinking Arts
Ethical Considerations
Moral Democracy

PREFACE

This is a summary of the philosophical system developed in the book, *The Immaterial Structure of Human Experience*. It serves as a key to the principal terms of the larger work by providing a brief definition for each concept without recourse to the extensive argumentation and development characteristic of the full exposition.

Key to the Philosophy of Immaterialism

There are **three purposes** for which this philosophy was developed. The **first** is that there is reason to believe that the universe might be composed of mind stuff. This is suggested by research in particle physics, where human awareness and experimental results appear to be interrelated.

No attempt will be made to go into this, as particle physics is a highly specialized field which lies outside the domain of this philosophy. It is sufficient to note that such a view places the old mechanistic interpretation of reality in doubt. The mechanistic perspective is not by any means obsolete. Rather it may be described as incomplete.

The **second** motive behind the development of this philosophy is that there is much in ordinary life which does not fall under a strictly material explanation. **Consciousness** is the single most important of the nonmaterial factors in human awareness. Can it be said that consciousness is merely an epiphenomenon of physiological events? Aside from this, do causal relations truly originate at the level of material perception? Answers to these questions cannot be strictly mechanistic in explanation.

The **third** motive arises from the nature of **value judgments**. What is their role in the development of human knowledge? In other words, can a strictly material explanation of reality account for the development of human understanding?

Key to the Philosophy of Immaterialism

What about the role of emotion in determining expressions of human yearning and motivation?

These guide the reasoning process. For in any such process the question may be asked, why is one logical train of thought pursued rather than another? Thus emotionally based value judgments are critical in the formation of rational structures. And, if emotions are critical in the formation of rational structures, can reason then be strictly relied upon to explain one sequence of emotions as opposed to another?

Science, particularly physical science, is empirical in character. Which is to say that it is phenomenally based. It relies upon a close observation of experimental results and an increasingly mathematical theoretical development. The latter satisfies **reason**. And the former references what is generally understood to be **sensory perception**.

But neither of them engages the heart, which is the domain of human yearning, valuation, and motivation. Thus, though science is of deep interest to any contemporary, educated person, scientism is repugnant to many. **Scientism** is the elevation of science into a religion. In so doing, it enters a domain of human experience for which it was never intended.

These considerations have led the present writer to a train of thought which, over a number of years, has culminated in a spiritual and therefore non-materialistic, or **immaterialist philosophy**. Such a philosophy may appear strange, as it did when the seventeenth century philosopher George Berkeley proposed something similar. But it has seemed necessary to fulfill the conditions listed above.

Not since the work of **Descartes** has it been possible to reach a satisfactory compromise between **mind** and **body**, **spirit** and **matter**. Though both have their proper domain of explanation, and may therefore be considered exclusive of one another, in either domain considerations of one or the other must predominate.

Accordingly, if both are to be considered together in the more comprehensive domain of philosophical thought, where such exclusiveness demands resolution, it is spirit which has been found to demonstrate the more inclusive view. So this is the perspective which dominates the following remarks.

Materialism is a closely related collection of beliefs which includes an objective existence of things that subsist independently of the person encountering such experience. This is the commonly accepted form of human experience. For people are inclined to believe that there is a physical world which is independent of their minds.

A **material viewpoint** entertains the perspective that there is an objective realm of things-in-themselves located in physical space and incremental time. Two of the most important characteristics of an objective material world are that material things exist in and of themselves, and that they are present when not observed by anyone. They also independently undergo a form of change which can be incrementally measured in terms of time.

A **thing-in-itself** is something which exists apart from human consciousness. In immaterialist philosophy there is no such thing. Apart from the mental experience of objects and events in an objective world, there should be something independent of human awareness or any other form of consciousness which supports their objective existence. Immaterialist philosophy does not accept this independent support. These objects and events only exist in consciousness.

Immaterialism is the philosophy that all experience occurs in the mind. Thus there is no objective thing-in-itself independent of the mind. This position undermines any argument for causal determinism. Causation must ultimately reside in some form of mind, or consciousness. Free will is therefore preserved, at least insofar as material experience is concerned.

In light of the view that all experience occurs in the mind and does not have a separate existence, it can be said that the universe is essentially consciousness, or mind. This consciousness is a condition for any kind of awareness, since consciousness is awareness. So any idea of an awareness which is greater, or more inclusive, than human consciousness is itself a form of consciousness.

Spirit is universal consciousness. There is but one universal spirit. Thus there is only one consciousness. Unlike material experience, pure consciousness, omitting any consideration of its content, is neither bounded nor divisible. It is not finite. It is therefore infinite, or "not finite," as just stated, the prefix "in" meaning "not.". Thus there can only be one consciousness: universal consciousness, or spirit. Hence all other forms of consciousness are individual expressions of the **self-limitation** of this one consciousness.

The limitations of a human consciousness are an expression of its content. Such content is determined by universal consciousness and uniquely experienced by each individual consciousness. Since there is only one consciousness, the uniqueness of each individual consciousness arises from the self-limitation of that one consciousness.

Primary mind is universal spirit, which in turn is universal consciousness, or universal awareness. Primary mind is universal because it encompasses all other forms of mind, or consciousness. Only a portion of what is known to primary mind is known to a more limited mind. **Secondary mind** is primary mind, or universal spirit, functioning in such a manner as to self-limit itself in order to present the human mind with a limited awareness. It does this by means of **focus**. Focus is the instrument of limitation. Any finite object is an object of limited focus. By employing focus through secondary mind, which is self-limited primary mind, primary mind is enabled to present the human mind with a limited awareness.

Human awareness is the content of the consciousness of an adult human being, exclusive of the subjective manner in which mental impressions are initially delivered to that awareness. A mature human awareness recognizes an objective realm. But it does not recognize the subjective origin of that objective realm.

Something which is **finite** is that which is bounded, or limited, in all of its characteristics. A **physical object**, or the **object of a thought**, is limited in both spatial dimension and time. There is nothing about it which is unlimited, or infinite. On the other hand, something which is **infinite** is in-finite, or not finite. Thus it is not bounded, or limited, in any of its characteristics. This does not include the indeterminately large or the indeterminately small. For these are finite entities which are indeterminate in some portion of their finitude.

For example: A number line is mistakenly said to be infinite. This is because a new number can be repeatedly added to it without end. But at any point at which the count is stopped, the length of the number line, and each of its components, is found to be finite. Thus the number line is indeterminate, rather than infinite. For infinite means not finite. If it was infinite, it would not be finite in any way.

Focus is the means by which universal spirit self-limits itself in order to produce a material consciousness. A material consciousness results from the limitation of its content. So it is for this purpose that focus becomes the source of the intuitions of **simple unity**, **plurality**, and **totality**. These intuitions render the human mind capable of recognizing and assimilating material experience.

The **intuition of simple unity** is the first of the three intuitions. It is the means by which a finite mind recognizes a unity. An example is one marble recognized as a distinct entity. Here focus limits conscious attention to those impressions on the mind which are the marble.

The **intuition of plurality** is the second of the three intuitions. It is the means by which the finite mind recognizes limitation, finitude, and plurality. An example involves a recognition of more than one marble in which each is observed in individual distinction from another. To recognize more than one marble is to recognize the limits of one in relation to the other. Hence the recognition of finitude and plurality.

The **intuition of totality** is the third of the three intuitions. A combination of the first two intuitions, it is the means by which the finite mind recognizes a unity of pluralities. An example would be a collection of five marbles recognized as a single collection. In this case, the second intuition is employed to recognize limitation and plurality. The first intuition then focuses attention on the collective plurality of individually limited entities by recognizing them together as a single group.

A **percept** is a mental impression. This constitutes the most basic element among the perceptual content of consciousness. Percepts form the whole of material awareness. To state that impressions on the mind are percepts does not imply the agency of the senses in rendering those impressions. Percepts are impressions directly perceived by the mind.

The **noumenal precipitate** is the means by which mental impressions (percepts) are registered in human consciousness. Due to focus, these percepts do not appear all at once. They appear in lineal sequence in the mind, as focus projects one after the other upon a human consciousness. Some percepts may be associated with others in the sequence, due to a repetition in proximity of appearance. The repetition of the same pattern enhances awareness of their associated appearance in the mind. There is no other organization among them.

The **phenomenal precipitate** results from an instantaneous transformation of the associated percepts of the noumenal precipitate into the extensions (objects) of mental and physical experience. These extensions may be objects of thought or physical objects. Insofar as they are understood to constitute physical objects, the percepts are **qualities** of the object.

Thus the human mind, undergoing an immediate experience of material impressions upon it, organizes the noumenally associated percepts into extensions. If the extensions are recognized as external perceptions, the mind further organizes them into physical space. As a result, these extensions become physical objects.

And the percepts composing those extensions become the qualities of physical objects. Otherwise, the mental objects are recognized as images, or extensions in the mind. These mental objects of thought resemble the physical inasmuch as they also are composed of percepts. But they are extended only in thought, rather than in physical space.

Subjective reality, in the most fundamental sense (which is that of the noumenal precipitate), is the awareness of percepts, generally but not always, in association with one another. It consists of impressions on the mind. Subjective reality may also be described as the realm of thought, feeling, and emotion, as opposed to the realm of physical objects and events.

Key to the Philosophy of Immaterialism

So there are two forms of subjectivity. The first is the noumenal precipitate, which generally becomes obscured to the adult mind as a result of the latter's complex workings at a practical level. The second is the subjectivity of thought, feeling, and emotion as opposed to physical objects and events. The second form of subjectivity, with its objective complement, is what has developed in a maturing mind at the expense of a continued recognition of the first form.

Objective reality is that portion of human experience in which objects and events appear in a physical context to have an existence independent of the will of the perceiver. This is due to the fact that objective things and events occur in an order which is independent of human action in varying degrees. In other words, the human mind is involved in constructing that world and in manipulating certain aspects of it. But the human will does not determine the behavior of all its elements or events.

Perception is the faculty involved in a recognition of material experience. One can be said to perceive a thought, a physical object, a physical event, or feelings. The term is generally used more narrowly to designate awareness of physical objects and events. Feelings, thoughts, objects, and events involve percepts, or impressions on the mind. Feelings and thoughts are considered subjective. Physical objects and events are considered objective.

All perceptions occur as impressions on the mind. If they are independent perceptions, they represent feelings. But many are associated together as extensions. These extensions form images in the mind, which either represent objects of thought or physical objects. Feelings, emotions (which are composed of feelings), and thoughts are subjective forms of mental life.

But when extensions are considered to be physical objects, their percepts are understood to be their qualities. For they are recognized as perceptions external to and independent of the mind. Thus the objects are experienced as existing in physical space. It is these objects, and the events which occur among them, that constitute physical experience.

So a **physical object** is understood to be an object of perception, rather than an object of thought (which is also perceived, but not as a physical object). A physical object is a physical extension which is experienced as existing in a contiguous relationship with other such extensions. The contiguity constitutes **physical space**.

In other words, a physical object is recognized as three dimensional. Two dimensions give it height and breadth. A third dimension gives it depth, or objective distance. And since it is understood to exist concurrently with other physical objects, they are three-dimensionally contiguous. This is what forms **space**. It is in this way that physical space becomes a greater extension which is a multiple of lesser extensions, or objects.

A explanation of the problem of an **empty space**, insofar as such a thing can be said to exist, is that an allowance is made by the mind for the imperfect fitting together of physical objects. For the **figure** (or shape) of physical objects is in part determined by internal properties. Thus contiguous physical extensions create a greater extension, which is physical space. But the extensions, or objects, are irregular in figure. So the gaps which occur between them are empty space.

A **mental extension** is a thought. There are two types of thoughts: **images** and **concepts**. A thought is extended in the mind because its object is an image which either represents a physical object, multiple objects, or something like these. For example, not only do the images and concepts "a man" and "men" refer to physical objects. The more abstract, general, and inclusive concept "mankind" must also, in final analysis, reference something physical, namely human beings.

Images are the essence of thought. For **concepts** are founded on **images**. They are a combination of images stabilized by a **definition** which specifies applicable properties. Even the word "abstract" can, when deliberatively accessed, supply the supporting imagery which constitutes its conceptual character. There is a sense of removing an idea from its concrete meaning. And that sense is represented by a pulling away or a lifting above. These are spatial extensions. Such images are always vaguely present, however disguised by the verbal expression.

A **mental object**, as an object of thought, represents the perceptual characteristics of a physical object, regardless of whether or not it is understood to exist as a physical object. Thus every thought involves an image, or set of images, however vaguely represented in the mind. For its properties may be hidden in a concept. Whereas they are clearly in view in imaginative expression.

But a thought is not understood to exist outside the mind in physical space. The difference between a mental and physical object lies in the attribution of subjectivity or objectivity. When a thought has an object taking the form of an image, the image is an extension. In this it resembles a physical object, which is also an extension.

But, whereas the physical extension (physical object) is experienced as existing in a contiguous relationship with other physical extensions, the mental object does not. It occupies **mental space**, where only one thought can appear in the mind at once. So thoughts are limited by sequence, but not by contiguity, since their objects do not exist in physical space. They are therefore subjective.

Key to the Philosophy of Immaterialism

Non-incremental time is time as it is expressed in the noumenal precipitate. This time is generally only consciously experienced in infancy or very early childhood, prior to a mature formation of the phenomenal precipitate. It arises as a consequence of the sequence in which mental focus introduces percept impressions to the mind. Because percepts are introduced sequentially in the noumenal precipitate, and because they do not individually exhibit dimensions, which are expressions of distance, this time cannot be measured. It is therefore not incremental.

Incremental time, on the other hand, is time as recognized in the phenomenal precipitate. It is the form of time experienced by a mature human awareness. It is determined incrementally by means of changes in a distance relationship between two extensions, one of which is undergoing change in relation to the other.

Such a changing distance relationship between two extensions is compared to another similar relationship, the first being held as a standard for demarking the other. It is a comparative measure of motion. Thus the movement of a hand, or change in digits (which latter also involves change in distance) on a stopwatch is used to time the performance of a sprinter. Incremental time can also be expressed in terms of a change within an extension, or object. This can be a chemical or physical change. It too involves motion, but within the object. So the same relations apply, but in a much subtler manner.

Incremental time is subjective only in the sense that it is objective time as measured by the subjective person. This person may note occurrences within his or herself in reference to objective events. However, true subjective time would be non-incremental. But in the mature mental life of a human being, this is obscured by the phenomenal precipitate.

Change is a condition which concerns an object whose relationship to other objects in physical space is altered. Or the qualities and, if it is a major change, the properties within it change. In either case, the change is a result of motion. For there is either external or internal movement. External motion occurs between one object and others. Internal motion involves a relation of parts within an object, however small that part may be which registers the change. Any motion involves a comparative change in distance.

Energy is the quantitative recognition and measure of change. Kinetic energy is the quantification of change in relation to stasis or to other changes. Potential energy is a quantified potential for change. These characteristics may be understood, and therefore observed, to occur in

Key to the Philosophy of Immaterialism

proportions which are consistently recognized. Thus the change and the relations of change, recognized in quantitative terms, are what is held to be energy.

A **representational viewpoint** is that viewpoint which considers the mind as producing an image or images within itself of whatever it is assumed to have perceived. In immaterialist philosophy, the thing perceived does not exist independently of the perceiver, but has its origin as an image in the mind. Thus it does not exist apart from its mental representation. It is that mental representation. Nonetheless, there can be a representation of the representation, as when a mental image is formed of what is assumed to have already been perceived.

The representational view treats physical objects and events as being objective. The **immaterial view** recognizes that all things and events occur as images in the mind (i.e., secondary mind, as opposed to common human awareness). However, this perspective blurs the distinction between subjectivity and an objective realm.

So the representational view alone is convenient for certain forms of discussion. It may even treat the external realm as entirely distinct from the internal. Though, in its acknowledged relation to immaterialist philosophy, it does not truly believe in this perspective because the immaterial view is more inclusive and takes philosophical precedence over it.

As stated previously, an association of percepts is a compact sequence of impressions in the noumenal mind. To be recognized as an association, the sequence must be closely repeated. When the percepts are transformed into an extension in the phenomenal mind, they become the representative characteristics of an object. When a specific type of percept, like the color red, is assumed to exist in a physical object, it is a quality. Combined qualities become **properties**.

An **image** is an association of mental impressions (percepts) which exhibits the qualities and properties of an object. It can be a mental representation interpreted as a perception. Or it can be recognized as independent of perception. Thus it may be a thought about a perception. But in some cases it may not represent any known physical object.

Whatever may be their circumstances, all mental images, perceptual and imaginative, employ percepts (mental impressions) which are understood to function as the qualities of objects, be they physical or merely mental objects. Accordingly, though an image can be formed which is not found in physical experience, its percepts can always be located in that experience. It is in this way that, while a unicorn is not known to physically exist, its properties do. Other objects may be entirely abstract and ideal, as in mathematics.

Key to the Philosophy of Immaterialism

Imagination is the image-forming faculty of the mind. Imagination underlies all processes of thought. For **concepts** are a unification of properties by means of a definition. These **properties** are represented by images. Now, imagination is a representational term. In the immaterialist perspective, images are directly inserted into human awareness by secondary mind. They are the associations of percepts.

Imaginative experience involves imaginative images which appear in the mind. All images appear only in the mind. But some are recognized as perceptions. These are not imaginative images in the commonly received sense of the term. But others are accepted as replicas of perceptions, while yet others are recognized as completely free associations of percepts. These latter kinds of image are both imaginative.

A **property** is a classificatory characteristic of a concept. Properties are composed of percepts, which are qualities in physical objects. They are registered in the mind as imagery representing an object of perception or an object of thought. Usually properties are associated in the plural, where they are what a definition organizes into the concept of an object.

A **definition** brings certain properties together within a concept, which is limited to them alone. The images within the concept can neither expand nor contract, leaving the concept rigidly defined. Whereas the properties of freely imagined objects of thought may expand or contract at will.

So a **concept** brings properties together and limits them by means of a definition. For concepts involve images, which represent the properties. Thus either images or other concepts which are supported by images constitute the properties. Nevertheless, it may seem as if a concept is distanced from its imagery. But this is not so. It is always supported by images.

A **classification** is an organization of properties into a concept by means of a definition. So a classification is a concept. Due to its specification of distinct properties, it has a nesting characteristic, which allows it to fully or partially include or exclude another classification.

Reason is a discipline of the mind by means of which concepts are brought together through a continuing transferral of meaning. That transferral of meaning is made possible by the nesting characteristic of concepts. To be sound reasoning, the transferral of meaning must follow the rules of logic. These are ultimately rules of imaginative association, which are limited by the inflexible character of the specific properties of the concepts involved.

In other words, underlying both the concepts employed and the rules of logic which bring them together in a transferral of meaning is the work of imagination. This work is limited by the inflexibility of the fixed properties of concepts. So it may be referred to as the work of disciplined imagination. Specifically, concepts are composed of images, which have been rendered inflexible by a definition. But underlying the logical relations between concepts are certain possible associative relationships between the images supporting them.

A **theoretical system** is a development of thought in which concepts are brought together in statements and statements are brought together in a system. Euclid's Elements is one such system. Darwin's argument for natural selection in *The Origin of Species* is another. Logical statements can be understood as single concepts. Entire systems can also be briefly stated as concepts. Thus concepts, logical statements, and systems are all classifications.

Concepts are incorporated within **logical statements**. For example, the subject and predicate of a proposition are brought together in a logical statement. Then logical statements are incorporated in a system by means of the rules of logic. Euclid's system depends upon proofs derived from axioms and theorems. Darwin's system depends upon a few broadly operative principles observed over a broad range of phenomena.

Intellectual experience involves concepts, statements, and theoretical systems. The statements and theoretical systems are formed from definitionally associated images representing properties within concepts. To state this in greater detail, it can be said that the human mind experiences images recognized as physical objects. From these object images, and from other imaginatively constructed images whose properties are drawn from the object images and recombined in new forms, the mind builds its intellectual view of reality.

As noted, it does this through associations which are made between the properties of the concepts. However, these associations are not as free as they would be in the unrestrained exercise of imagination. Rather, they are developed in accordance with logical rules. The rules require that the associative relations between properties should be carried out in view of the restrictions imposed by definitional limits upon the concepts.

It is in this way that logical thinking results in statements and the theoretical systems constructed from these statements. It is thinking disciplined by logical procedure. But, to be

Key to the Philosophy of Immaterialism

creative, it must also involve imaginative input. Hence the role of the imaginatively constructed images whose properties are drawn from object images and recombined into new concepts, which are then associatively incorporated in the system by means of logical procedure.

A **feeling** is a percept (mental impression) which is not associated with other percepts. Because it does not form an association, or extension, a feeling is not a physical object. Nor is it an object of thought. It is strictly subjective and does not form an image in the mind.

An **emotion** is a coalescence of percepts of feeling. There is more than one kind of feeling involved in an emotion. A coalescence of percepts is not an association of percepts. Thus the percepts of feeling are recognized individually. Together they form an emotion composed of clearly articulated individual feelings of different kinds.

A **coalescence of percepts** is a series of impressions on the mind (i.e., percepts) which are not recognized as associated with one another, but in which a close sequential occurrence of impressions is recognized. An emotion is composed of an alternately repeated sequence of different feelings.

Memory is experienced as a mental record of past experience. However, in immaterialist philosophy no such record exists physically. Rather, impressions of past experience are repeated in the mind at times which are appropriate for the functioning of memory. Whereas, in materialism memory is associated with brain function, in immaterialist philosophy this bodily reference must be considered a correspondence of representations in the mind. For example, a memory might appear to be recalled by a present physical or mental stimulus. But these do not recall it. They coincide with it. It is in this way that the representations of memory occur in association with events.

www.ingramcontent.com/pod-product-compliance
Lightning Source LLC
Chambersburg PA
CBHW050048080526
44586CB00014B/1511